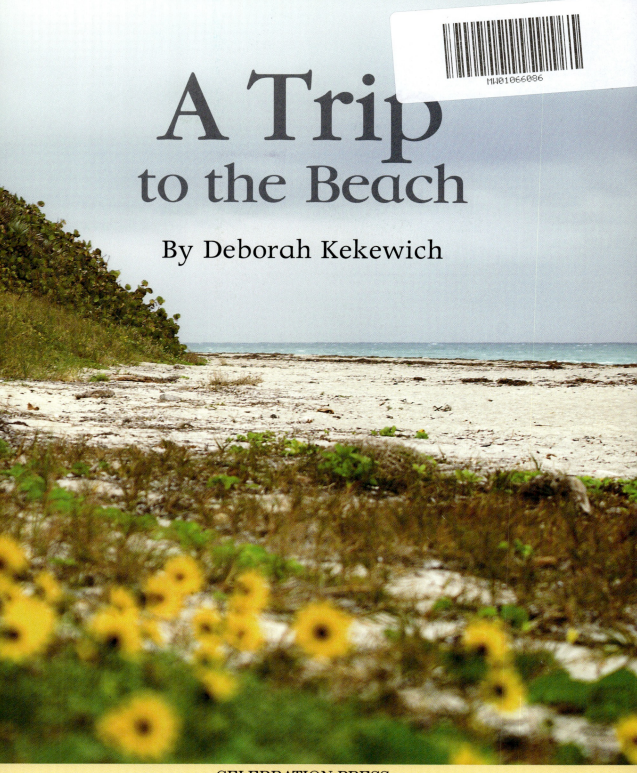

A Trip
to the Beach

By Deborah Kekewich

CELEBRATION PRESS
Pearson Learning Group

My family went to the beach.

It was too cold to swim.

We explored the beach.

sea star

sea gull

fish

We found animals
near the water.

crab

Dad found an animal
in the sand.

clams

snail

barnacles

My brother found animals
along the shoreline.

We had a great day
at the beach!